STRONG IN THE LORD

MEN'S GROUP BIBLE STUDY

WRITTEN BY Jim Kane

Strong in the Lord: Men's Group Bible Study
Written by Jim Kane
© 2019 Warner Press Inc.

Requests for information should be sent to:
Warner Press Inc.
P.O. Box 2499
Anderson, IN 46018
www.warnerpress.org

Kevin Stiffler • Editor
S. Katie Miller • Layout & Design

CONTENTS

The Warner Press *Relevance* Group Bible Studies provide intriguing examinations of topics using the whole of the Scriptures. The guides incorporate various stories and activities to introduce and apply the subject matter, with a Bible study component at the heart of each session. Our goal is to show life-long believers and those new to the faith how to know the Lord intimately while encouraging them to step out and join him in his work with miraculous results.

These flexible studies are ideal for any setting. We know that time is a valuable commodity in today's society, and that's why each book consists of five or six short lessons intended to meet the group's scheduling needs.

You Can Fight the Good Fight

1 Corinthians 10:1–13

Main Point

Times of temptation will come, but God is faithful to provide endurance and a way out.

Background

Two of the Epistles written by the apostle Paul were to the believers in Corinth, which was a metropolitan city located in the country of Greece. Paul addressed several problems in the church that were causing division, arguments, and a lack of spiritual growth and maturity. In 1 Corinthians 10, Paul reminded the Corinthian Christians, many of whom were likely converts from Judaism, of what had happened to their ancestors when they failed to obey the Lord. Paul's words caution that we should not be smug in the life of faith. When we face temptation, God is faithful to provide what we need so that we do not fall.

Power in Christ

A fellow employee whom you have gotten to know better over the past two years confides in you that he has been lying to his live-in fiancé about spending money. He tells her that he buys lunch at work each day, but he is really using the money to purchase lottery tickets. Over time he has lost several thousand dollars in this way. He admits that he has had a gambling problem in the past, which cost him a job and a previous relationship. You and this coworker have never discussed faith matters, but he is desperate for help.

How would you share with your coworker that he can have the power to stop? Is this an appropriate point to bring up the gospel, or would it be best to just suggest common-sense measures for dealing with his compulsive behavior and his fiancé? Why?

What principles from God's Word would be helpful for someone in this situation?

I. Read 1 Corinthians 10:1–5.

What did the ancient Israelites do that caused them to die in the desert?

____

____

____

God's ancient people had all they needed for righteous living, but they blew it. How do people today squander opportunities to live in intimate fellowship with God?

____

____

____

____

II. Read 1 Corinthians 10:6–10.

What did Paul hope his current readers would learn from the mistakes of their ancestors?

____

____

____

____

In your own words, what does it look like today to be an idolater? to commit
sexual immortality? to test Christ? to grumble?

____

____

____

____

____

III. Read 1 Corinthians 10:11–13.

What do you think it means that "the culmination of the ages" had come on
Paul's readers—including us? How does this make you feel and why?

____

____

____

Modern technology—including videos, the Internet, cell phones, transpor-
tation, and electronic payments—provide easy access to an endless variety
of temptations. Is Paul's assertion that the temptations we face are common
to all human beings still true? Explain.

____

____

____

How do you feel when you give in to temptation? Why are we subject to temptation, and what gives temptation its power?

How is God faithful when it comes to not letting us be tempted beyond what we can bear? How can we cooperate with the Lord in living out this truth? How can a group such as this one be an effective tool for beating temptation?

Does God sometimes use interruptions to keep us from being tempted beyond what we can bear? Explain. What other methods does God use?

Practically speaking, what does "a way out" of temptation look like? Describe at least three ways God might provide endurance through or a way out of a tempting situation. How do we recognize a way out or assess that we have the endurance to make it through?

How have you taken a way out when a temptation has come your way? Briefly describe the experience.

What other advice have you read or heard regarding how to get away from temptation? How does this line up with Paul's words here?

How does prayer help with finding and taking a way out or enduring temptation?

Which aspect of temptation do you find the hardest to battle: the mental aspect (thoughts, fantasies); the emotional aspect (specific feelings such as loneliness, anger); or the spiritual aspect (feeling unworthy of God's love)? Why? What might a "way out" look like for one of these aspects?

What makes some people a source of reliable help for beating temptation? Do you have such people in your life? If not, how could you connect with such people?

Cause and Effect

"The Devil made me do it!" This somewhat tongue-in-cheek statement is sometimes used as an excuse when someone gets caught doing something bad. But James wrote about the real reason we fall into sin: "Each person is tempted when they are dragged away by their own evil desire and enticed. Then, after desire has conceived, it gives birth to sin; and sin, when it is full-grown, gives birth to death" (James 1:14–15). The description of being dragged away is very appropriate. When we set our desires on something bad, the pull is strong. Once we give in and have entered into sin, death is the inevitable result. But we don't have to travel this road that leads to our own destruction.

List examples of public figures whose sin led to downfall and heartache. What was the outcome? How did they explain their behavior? What can we learn from their experience?

____

____

____

____

____

Why do some things seem to be a major temptation for some people but no temptation at all for others?

____

____

Planning for Victory

In reflecting on his life of service to God, Paul said that he had "fought the good fight" (2 Tim 4:7). One way to "fight the good fight" with respect to temptation is to have a plan to face it. Here is a visual to help construct such a plan. Think about three circles, one inside another inside another:

The *inner* circle represents specific habits or things that you know you have to stay away from. For example, maybe overeating has been a problem for you.

The *middle* circle represents "triggers"—situations that tempt you to use your inner-circle habits or things to cope. For example, maybe pressure at work tempts you to overeat as a way of coping.

The *outer* circle represents ways of resisting temptation. For example, maybe you have an accountability partner you can talk to when you are under pressure at work and tempted to overeat.

For the inner circle, what are two or three major temptations you want to avoid? For the middle circle, what are two or three triggers that cause you give in to these temptations? For the outer circle, what are two or three things you can use to help you resist temptation?

The Power of Accountability

If you were in the emergency room, there are probably at least a couple of people you would want to know you were there. How about when you are battling temptation? Who would you want to "be in the know" and provide support for you?

Remember, today's text is from a letter Paul wrote to a *group* of people—the Corinthian church—and not to an individual or isolated believer. Part of the "way out" of temptation the Lord provides us is having a group of people who will listen to us, offer some suggestions, and pray with us.

In the space below, write down the names of three other men who you think would be good sources of accountability for you:

____

____

____

Consider reaching out to these men and asking them if they would be willing for you to contact them when you are struggling with temptation or just as a way of staying true to God during the day. Would this be easy or difficult to do? Why?

____

____

____

Closing Prayer

Lord God, we need your help to resist temptation. We need your strength to say no. And as hard as it may be to acmit, we need other people to help us stay strong and be victorious. Help us commit to this journey of accountability. Help us to let go of our pride and self-sufficiency, for they have not helped us be victor ous. Help us to be honest with at leas one other man about our temptations and struggles. Amer.■

You Can Understand God's Word

Joshua 1:1–11

Main Point

God's Word to us, the Bible, is important for helping us grow in our faith; the Lord wants us to understand and follow it.

Background

As the Israelites prepared to enter the Promised Land, the Lord gave Joshua words of direction and encouragement. Joshua had become the new leader when Moses died. Along with Joshua, a new generation of people would now take possession of what had been promised long ago. Years earlier, Joshua had expressed confidence that God's people could conquer the Promised Land. But now that Moses was gone, perhaps Joshua felt some uncertainty about his own capabilities. How could he lead as God expected? Obeying God's Law and meditating on it would give Joshua the strength and courage he needed. And God would be faithful to grant the promised success.

Big Shoes to Fill

You have been hired as a new supervisor at a new employer after having been at your former job for ten years. The supervisor you are replacing has just retired and had been with the company for twenty-five years, the past fifteen of these as head of the department you have hired into. This team has been functioning well and your predecessor was well loved and respected. The company has just launched a new product line that your department will be strategically involved in producing. The team, and your boss, are understandably nervous and are looking to you for leadership. The production manual for the new product line was created and tested at other company locations overseas and was co-written by the manufacturer of the machines to be used in the new product line.

How strictly would you follow the production manual, and why? What might be its limitations?

What other resources besides the production manual might be helpful in successfully making this new product line?

What pressures, expectations, and other factors might influence your response and performance as a new leader in this situation?

I. Read Joshua 1:1–6.

The Lord seemed pretty blunt in outlining the situation for Joshua. How do you think Joshua felt in taking on this leadership assignment? What past evidence do we have that Joshua was a devoted follower of the Lord and a passionate believer in God's promises?

What threats and challenges—from outside the nation and from within it—would have caused Joshua to need a good dose of God's strength and courage?

II. Read Joshua 1:7–9.

What does "Book of the Law" (v 8) refer to? Why would it mean for Joshua to keep the Book of the Law "on his lips"? What was in the Book of the Law that Joshua needed to know?

For Christians, what is the "Book of the Law"? How do we keep it "on our lips"?

____

____

____

What does it mean to meditate on something? What does it mean specif-ically to meditate on the Book of the Law? How would this be helpful to Joshua? How can it be helpful to us?

____

____

____

____

____

What does it mean to "be careful" in doing what is written in the Book of the Law? How does this requirement apply to us today? Is it even possible to do _everything_ written in the Bible? Explain.

____

____

____

____

What kind of prosperity and success come to those who faithfully keep God's Word? Is this some sort of financial blessing, or something else? Explain.

What seems to be the link between the success God promised in verses 1–6, obedience to God, and the knowledge and understanding of the Book of the Law?

Why is the presence of God a promise that should give us strength and courage?

When have you seen a leader boldly step forward in God's strength and be used by God to do great things? When have you seen a leader's lack of courage result in a lack of progress? Aren't all leaders in God's kingdom called to be strong and courageous? Why do some seem to experience great success in doing the Lord's work while others seem to struggle?

____

____

____

____

Why does the success of most groups (whether or not those groups are faith-based) so often depend on the capabilities and success of the human leaders of those groups?

____

____

____

____

III. Read Joshua 1:10–11.

What evidence do we see here that Joshua trusted in God's help and that the encouragement God provided had accomplished its purpose?

____

____

____

Who, What, When, Where, and Why

Good Bible study takes into consideration the context of the passage being considered. *Eisegesis* means to interpret a text in such a way that we introduce our own presuppositions, agendas, or biases into the text. The misunderstanding and misapplication of God's Word have been used in the past to justify slavery and the oppression of women. In studying a passage, it is good to ascertain the context by seeking to discover things such as who was speaking (or writing), who was listening (or reading), when the passage was written, why the passage was written, etc.

Go back and read Joshua 1:5b–9 again. Who was speaking in this passage, and who was listening?

____

____

____

What is the main point of what was being said? What is important about this point?

____

____

____

____

Why were the things said here important at that particular time to the person who heard them? By extension, why were they important to the people of Israel at that point in their journey?

Interpreting and Applying

Two important yet difficult things to do for effective Bible study are *interpretation* and *application*, to determine the meaning of what we read and understanding how we should respond. Think about Joshua 1:5b–9 again. You have already considered what God's words meant for Joshua and the Israelites at that time. But now think about how the passage transcends time and speaks to our lives now.

Why were these words spoken, written down, and preserved across the centuries for us to read today?

What is God's main point to us? What does God want us to do? What do you take away from this passage?

Based on this passage, what do you believe God is calling you to do *right now*?

____

____

____

____

Describe a time you faced a period of fear or uncertainty. What did you do to get through that time? How might the things you have learned in today's study make a difference in the way you face such times in the future?

____

____

____

____

____

____

____

What passage did you pick, and why? Is there something that drew you to it?

Even if this passage has already been a blessing or encouragement to you, how might your familiarity with it prevent you from seeing something in it you did not see before?

For the passage you chose, who was speaking (or writing), and who was listening (or reading)? What is the main point of what was being said? What is important about this point? Why were the things said important at that particular time to the person(s) who heard them?

Why were the words of this passage written down and preserved across the centuries for us to read today? What is God's main point to us in this passage? What does God want us to do? What do you believe God is calling you to do *right now*?

____

____

____

____

____

Closing Prayer

Lord, your Word is a lamp for our feet and a light on our path, making us strong and courageous. We need your guidance each day to know and do what is right. Take us deeper in the study, understanding, and application of your Word. Help us to grasp the truth we encounter so that we might become mature followers and disciples of and for you. Thank you for the gift of the Bible to us. Amen. ■

L3

You Can Be Successful

Matthew 25:14–30

Main Point

In a society in which success is worshipped and sought after, we are called to be faithful to God and to be faithful with the blessings God has given us.

Background

Our text for today is the Parable of the Bags of Gold, a part of Jesus' discourse with the disciples in the final days before his arrest and crucifixion. On either side of the passage are other parables that also describe what the kingdom of heaven is like. God expects us to use the gifts and abilities we have to be faithful in our service; in fact, we will one day be asked to give account for what we have (or haven't) done with what we have been given. Citizens of God's kingdom are called to be faithful and to be prepared.

Famous Last Words

Even if we were to consider what our last words in this life might be, none of us can be certain of those words because none of us know when the end of this life will come. Some people's last words seem profound, others not so much. Here are the reported last words of a few famous people:

- "Oh wow. Oh wow. Oh wow." —Steve Jobs, to his family
- "I'm bored with it all." —Sir Winston Churchill
- "Nancy, I want you to know my last thoughts are of you." —P. T. Barnum, to his wife
- "I want nothing but death." —Jane Austen, to her sister
- "This is the last of earth. I am content." —John Quincy Adams

Which statement do find most interesting? Why? If you know anything about any of the people who said these things, do their words reflect the lives they lived? Explain. Which of these final words seem to reflect some kind of faith in or awareness of God?

Have you ever heard someone utter his or her final words? If so, what were they? What do you think might be your own last words? Why?

I. Read Matthew 25:14–18.

Jesus was teaching here about the kingdom of heaven (the "it" he referred to in verse 14). Was he talking about some future point in time or life now? Explain. In what ways is God's kingdom like a man setting off on a journey and entrusting his wealth to his servants?

Do you think the servants' task of putting the master's money to work was a special assignment to carry out while he was away, or was it their "regular" job? Explain.

What might have been the feelings of the servants as they received the gold, assuming they each knew what the others received? Why? How would you have felt at receiving the five bags of gold? at receiving the single bag of gold?

____

____

____

____

II. Read Matthew 25:19–27.

In what ways do servants share in the happiness of their master? In what ways do we share in the happiness of God?

____

____

____

____

What reason did the third servant give for hiding his bag of gold in the ground? Did his master's response confirm or contradict the servant's feelings? Explain.

____

____

____

Is God a "hard" master—one who harvests and gathers in unreasonable ways? Why or why not?

How would you have felt if you were one of the first two servants and were present when the third servant was reprimanded? Why?

III. Read Matthew 25:28–30.

In this parable, what do the bags of gold represent? What does the journey taken by the owner of the gold represent?

In what ways have you seen those who already have a lot get more with seemingly little or no effort, while those who have little seem to easily lose what they do have?

With what does God entrust us, and why? What is the point of different people receiving different amounts of gold?

Which servant do you most identify with? Why?

Describe someone you know who has been faithful with a few things. What was the motivation for his or her faithfulness? How has that faithfulness been recognized or rewarded?

____

____

____

____

If this is how life is (and will be) in God's kingdom, how well do you think most believers are doing with the things God has entrusted to them? Why? Looking at our own lives, how do we evaluate how well we are doing with the things God has entrusted to us? What are the standards for measurement?

____

____

____

____

____

____

In Sickness and in Health

Lynda became a believer at an early age. She was married after college, eventually taking a job as a bookkeeper. One day at work, she lost her balance and fell, but she couldn't get up; her legs wouldn't move. In the hospital, she received a diagnosis of multiple sclerosis. Her health deteriorated quickly to the point where she needed constant care, unable even to feed herself.

In many marriages where one spouse develops MS, the other one leaves, unable to cope with the drastic changes that are occurring. But Lynda and her husband were both empowered by the love of God and a love for each other. They remained true to God and true to the vows they had made to each other in God's sight.

What strikes you about this story regarding faithfulness? Do you believe there were moments when that faithfulness was tested? What might have kept it alive? What does this say about the importance of faithfulness?

Think of one of the "bags of gold" God has given us as relationships—at home, at work, in the church and community. What, then, does today's parable have to say about being faithful in this area of life?

Faithful at Work

You are the parent of a high school student who has just been hired for her first part-time job at a local store. Over the first month you watch her grow (and struggle) as she learns how to be a good and faithful worker despite the demands of her schedule and the constant pull by some of her friends to skip work. But she settles down into a routine and soon is a productive and valuable employee.

One day your daughter comes homes in tears and in shock about a situation at work. A couple of her friends took some merchandise in plain view without paying for it as she was closing the store for the evening. There were no other co-workers present at the time.

How would today's parable be applicable to help your daughter to do the right thing in this situation? What would you want her to learn about being faithful to God, to her employer, to her friends, and to herself?

How do these changes offer new perspectives on what Jesus was trying to teach about faithfulness? How do things change depending on whether we are on the giving or receiving end of faithfulness?

In today's text, Jesus used a parable to help teach the disciples what the kingdom of heaven is like. What do we learn about our own faithfulness to God? about our faithfulness to others (and their faithfulness to us) in human relationships?

Closing Prayer

God, faithfulness seems to be in short supply these days. We often struggle with our own faithfulness, as numerous temptations to satisfy our own desires and habits challenge our commitments to family, friends, work, the church, and you. We need your strength and power, knowing that one day we will give an account as to how faithful we were with what you gave us. Forgive us for our unfaithfulness and strengthen us to be faithful men. Amen.■

L4

You Can Be a Leader

Exodus 18:13–26

Main Point

Leadership is a vital function in life and ministry. There are various kinds of leaders, but good leaders share responsibility and empower others to lead and serve as well.

Background

Moses' father-in-law, Jethro, came to visit Moses and his family. While he was there, he saw the leadership overload that Moses was carrying. Expressing his concern about the stress and pressure Moses was under, he suggested a way for Moses to reduce his workload by sharing the leadership with a wider group of men who would help in resolving disputes among the people. Those situations that could not be decided at lower levels would be sent up to be adjudicated by Moses. This charge would lighten Moses' load considerably, so that he would not have to spend all his waking hours working, and also provide for more effective leadership.

Preparing to Lead

You are a member of the Parent-Teacher Organization for your children's school and there is a need for someone to give leadership to the biggest fundraiser of the year—a carnival. The outgoing leader has done it for five years, during which time the event has grown tremendously and been successful by most measures. But there is some concern that this leader did not really delegate many responsibilities for the carnival, doing most of the major work herself.

You agree to lead the carnival for the next year, and there will be five months for you to prepare. When you meet with the outgoing leader, there are a few minutes of casual pleasantries. But then she pulls out a large set of paper files and a flash drive containing spreadsheet information and places them on the table. She says, "Good luck! I hope you can make it happen next fall!" And she leaves.

What are the first few steps you would take to get organized? What kind of team would you put together?

Are you an effective delegator, or do you tend to try to do all the work yourself, even in situations where others are available and expected to help?

I. Read Exodus 18:13–16.

Moses led a group of millions of people (Ex 12:37). How many disputes do you think he had to deal with in a day? What kinds of disputes might these have been? Why do you think the people consistently looked to Moses to settle their disputes?

____

____

____

____

Why do you think Jethro commented on Moses' work style? What did he see that concerned him? How might Moses have been feeling at this point?

____

____

____

____

What do you make of Moses' seeming confidence in his abilities to decide between the parties in these disputes and communicate God's will in each matter? Did he display a failure to properly delegate authority, or was something else at play here? Explain.

____

____

____

II. Read Exodus 18:17–23.

What does it mean for someone to be a "representative before God" (v 19)?

Summarize Jethro's suggestion for how Moses should modify his leadership system. Was it a good suggestion? What was Jethro's goal in making this suggestion?

Why do you think it had not yet occurred to Moses to delegate some of the responsibility of acting as judge for the people?

If you have ever been told (or recognized on your own) that you were over-loaded as a leader, describe the situation. How did you feel? How did things turn out? What are some signs that a leader is likely approaching burnout from trying to do too much?

____

____

____

____

Why is it important to teach people the rules, laws, policies, or procedures of a group, a city, a nation, or another organization? How can this help to "lighten the load" of court cases?

____

____

____

____

What were the criteria Jethro advised for those Moses would choose to help as judges? What are the benefits of having these standards for leaders in the church, in politics, and in other areas?

____

____

____

Jethro advised a sort of "court hierarchy" or tiered system of judges, with Moses as the "supreme court." This is how our court system is set up today. What do you think of this system? Does it work? Are people able to get a fair and speedy trial? Explain.

III. Read Exodus 18:24–26.

What was the result of Moses listening to Jethro? Do you believe this was a God-honoring and appropriate system for the Israelites? What were some of the possible barriers Moses had to overcome for this change to take place? What barriers might the people have had to overcome?

Developing Leaders

You are a member of your congregation's leadership team, which is discussing how to reorganize the church's ministry structure. The pastor has traditionally been involved in all aspects of leadership at the church, and the goal is to allow him to devote more time to leadership development, preaching, and teaching. The team has looked at several options of ministry models and narrowed the choices down to two. One option is to organize along age-level lines with three teams: children, youth, and adults. The other option is to organize along three operational lines: evangelism, discipleship, and service. A major part of either scenario will be the recruitment of volunteers to provide leadership in the three areas.

Which of the two ministry models would you choose, and why?

____

____

____

How would you use today's study passage to encourage your pastor and the leadership team to keep the pastor and themselves from being overburdened and to allow others to serve, regardless of which ministry model is chosen?

____

____

____

Leadership Styles

Consultant Richard Martin suggests that leadership styles may be labeled as Tactical, Strategic, or Operational. Tactical leaders focus on getting something done by selecting and developing the correct plan of action. Decisions are made for short-term or immediate gains. Strategic leaders focus on the big picture and the long-term performance of an organization. Mission and vision are seen as very important. Operational leaders focus on the systems and methods needed to help the organization meet its goals. High motivation and high morale tend to be cultivated. All three kinds of leadership are necessary and important for an organization to grow and thrive.

Which of these three kinds of leadership is most talked about and stressed today? Why? Which kind of leader are you most like?

Do you think there is too much emphasis on one kind of leadership over the others? Explain.

What kind of leader does today's passage describe Moses as being? Why do you say so?

Describe the ministry you would develop. Why is this so important to you?

____

____

____

____

Write a brief mission statement for the ministry.

____

____

____

____

As the leader of this ministry, how would you go about getting other leaders in place?

What do you hope to accomplish in the first year with this ministry? How about in three years?

What have you learned about leadership from today's study that will help you in your leadership role?

Do you think leaders are made or born? Explain.

Closing Prayer

God, we struggle sometimes to see ourselves as leaders because we feel that we don't necessarily have the personality traits of a leader. But we all fill some leadership roles, whether or not they are paid or "official" positions. With your guidance and knowledge, we can be effective leaders in our homes, churches, and places of work. Help us to embrace the skills and gifts we have been given and to lead for your honor and glory. Amen.■

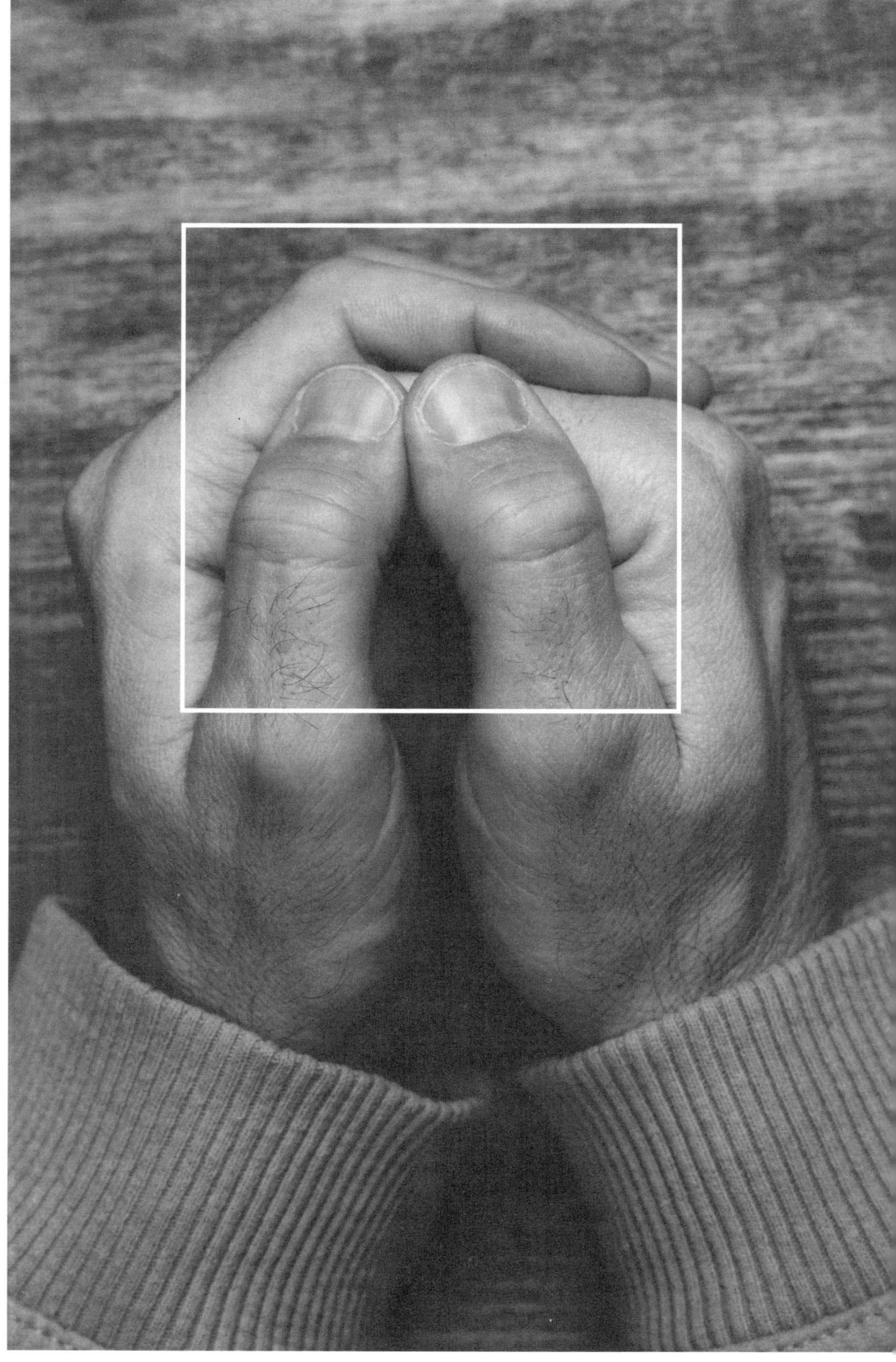

You Can Pray

Philippians 4:4–9

Main Point

Prayer matters in many ways, and we should pray about every situation we face.

Background

When Paul wrote to the believers in the ancient city of Philippi, he reminded them that their anxiety was best dealt with by praying "in every situation" with gratitude to God. This emphasis on prayer included encouragement to rejoice, to think on and about those things that are good and right, with the promise of God's presence and peace. These words of instruction, challenge, and encouragement are for the church today as well. When rejoicing, gentleness, dependence on God, and a focus on positive things dominate our lives, anxiety fades. Perhaps the best result of prayer is not the direct answer to our requests but the peace that comes from it.

Talking to Jesus

A dying man told his pastor that prayer was something he had never really embraced until one day a friend told him to place an empty chair beside his bed and talk to it as if Jesus were sitting in the chair. The man had found this to be a very helpful way to pray.

Several days later the man's daughter called the pastor and informed him that her father had passed away. The pastor asked if the gentleman had died in peace. She said that he did. They had enjoyed a wonderful conversation before she left for the grocery store. And when she returned home an hour later, she found that her dad had passed—with his head laying on the empty chair.

What does this story say to you about prayer? Do you find it hard to pray? Why or why not?

Do you think it can be more difficult for men to pray than for women? Why or why not?

What do you want to learn from this lesson on prayer?

I. Read Philippians 4:4–5.

What did Paul mean about the Lord being near? That Jesus lives in our hearts? That the Holy Spirit is with us? That Jesus is coming back soon? Or something else? Explain.

____

____

____

What might the Lord being near have to do with rejoicing? What might it have to do with being gentle?

____

____

____

II. Read Philippians 4:6–7.

Anxiety is a major issue that affects men as well as women. Sometimes medication is prescribed to help people deal with their anxiety. But how can prayer help? Was Paul referring to another kind of anxiety that does not require medication? Explain.

____

____

____

____

Does taking medication or going to counseling to help with anxiety demonstrate a lack of faith in God? Why or why not?

What do you do when you are anxious? How has prayer helped?

To petition is to appeal to someone for resolution. Paul encouraged the Philippian Christians to pray and appeal to the Lord *in every situation*. What does that mean? Is anything off limits from prayer? Explain.

Are there any situations in which prayer is not necessary? If so, what are they? If not, why not?

What is the relationship between thanksgiving and prayer? How does thanksgiving enable prayer? How does prayer enable thanksgiving?

III. Read Philippians 4:8–9.

Today and even in years past, some preachers have been criticized for what has been labeled a "feel-good" or overly optimistic presentation of the gospel: just think positively and everything will turn out okay. Is this the kind of message Paul was presenting here? Explain. What is the proper role of "positive thinking" in the life of a believer? What are the benefits?

How could Paul hold himself up as an example of someone whose teaching the Philippian believers should follow? Would you offer your own life as an example to others of how to live faithfully for the Lord? When others listen to your words or observe your actions, what do they learn about the God you follow?

____

____

____

____

____

In the NIV Bible, this section of Paul's letter is subtitled "Final Exhortations"— in other words, Paul really wanted his readers to remember and do these things. Why are the things Paul wrote here important for believers to know and do? If you were speaking what may be your last words to your family members and loved ones, what are the important things you would want them to know and remember? Why?

____

____

____

____

____

A Model for Prayer

One useful model for prayer is based on the term *ACTS*, as follows:

A stands for *Adoration.* To adore someone is to love and care for that person for who he or she is, not based on performance. Prayer should include praising God for who God is, not just for what God has done.

C stands for *Confession.* To confess in prayer is to admit the truth about our sin and shortcomings and seek God's mercy. This helps us grow in our faith as we practice honesty before God.

T stands for *Thanksgiving*. To give thanks is to express gratitude for God's blessings, salvation. strength, and help. Thanksgiving is a great antidote to fear, anxiety, and other issues we deal with. God deserves our thanks.

S stands for *Supplication.* An older word, supplication means to earnestly plead for or on behalf of someone or something. Prayer is our way of lifting others up to God for God's intervention and help

Do you find this to be a useful model for prayer? Explain. What other models have you heard of?

Which of these four elements do you need to implement more in your prayer life? Why?

____

____

____

____

____

Praying the Scriptures

An ancient practice of prayer that is still used by many today is called *Lectio Divina*, or "Divine Reading." Simply explained, it involves praying the Scriptures. Here are more details on how it works:

1. Select a few Bible verses, and designate a time and place for quiet reflection.

2. Read through the verses, listening for a word or phrase that jumps out at you. Take some moments of silence to recite or ponder the word or phrase.

3. Read the verses a second time as you continue to meditate on the word or phrase you have identified. Consider how this word or phrase is touching your life today.

4. As you read the verses a final time, consider how God is calling you to take action or make a change through this passage.

Pray Philippians 4:6–7 using these guidelines. What word or phrase did you identify? How is it impacting your life and calling you to change?

Perspectives on Prayer

Read through the following quotes about prayer:

"I have been driven many times upon my knees by the overwhelming conviction that I had nowhere else to go. My own wisdom and that of all about me seemed insufficient for that day."
— attributed to Abraham Lincoln

"We tend to use prayer as a last resort, but God wants it to be our first line of defense. We pray when there's nothing else we can do, but God wants us to pray before we do anything at all." —Oswald Chambers

"Is prayer your steering wheel or your spare tire?" —Corrie Ten Boom

"I have so much to do that I shall spend the first three hours in prayer." —Martin Luther

"We should seek not so much to pray, but to become prayer." —Francis of Assisi

Which of these quotes come the closest to your current thinking about prayer? Why?

What have you learned about prayer in this session?

____

____

____

____

____

Closing Prayer

Lord, sometimes we struggle to know what to say when we come to you in prayer. Our hearts and minds get so murky that they cloud our speech, and anxiety fills our thoughts. But we believe you know what we are trying to say, and we trust that you really do hear us. We are grateful that you are a God who listens to us, providing peace that guards our hearts and minds. In this we rejoice. Amen.■

You Can Be Fruitful

Galatians 5:16–26

Main Point

As disciples of Christ, we are called to a change of character from self-centered, indulgent living to lives filled with the fruit of the Holy Spirit.

Background

In writing to the Christians in Galatia, Paul encouraged these believers to become mature and to grow in their faith. The life of faith is one of freedom, but the purpose of this freedom is to serve others rather than gratify the self. There is a definite contrast between a life lived as a slave to the flesh (human nature) and a life lived in the Spirit; in fact, they are opposites. Those who keep in step with the Spirit will display the fruit of the Spirt in their lives. These characteristics clearly set apart the lives of those who stand to inherit the kingdom of God.

Apples and Oranges

The definition of *fruit* is the seed-bearing structure of flowering plants. Things such as apples, bananas, grapes, lemons, oranges, and strawberries clearly fit the description. But cucumbers, pumpkins, and tomatoes are also technically fruits. Plants grow fruit so they can propagate. Humans and many animals depend on fruit as a source of food. People cultivate plants so they can eat the fruit, which helps to ensure the survival and spread of the plants. Fruit accounts for a sizeable portion of the world's agricultural production.

In speaking about gauging the validity of those who claim to be prophets, Jesus said, "By their fruit you will recognize them" (Matt 7:16a). Why do you think he chose this particular word-picture to illustrate his point? What is the "fruit" in the life of a prophet or the life of anyone else?

What kind of fruit do you exhibit in your daily life? Is it God-honoring? Why or why not?

I. Read Galatians 5:16–18.

The original Greek of the New Testament was written in all capital letters, so it was up to translators to determine when it was appropriate to capitalize a word. How do we know Paul was referring to the Holy Spirit here and not the "small-*s*" spirit of human beings?

What did Paul mean by "the flesh"? Was he talking about our physical bodies, our character, or something else? Why do you say so?

Why are the desires of the flesh at odds with the Spirit?

What did Paul mean when he said that we are not under the law? What law was he referring to?

What does it mean to be led by the Spirit? Why is important to be led by the Spirit? Are you currently being led by the Spirit? If so, how? If not, why not?

II. Read Galatians 5:19–21.

Why did Paul call these things "acts of the flesh"? Describe what each of these acts looks like in our society today. Now, rank them in order from least bad to absolute worst from your own perspective. Why did you choose as you did?

Do you think God ranks these "acts of the flesh"? If so, why? If not, why not?

____

____

____

Why can't those whose lives exhibit these "acts of the flesh" inherit God's kingdom?

____

____

____

Which of these acts do you struggle with the most? the least? How are these acts overcome?

____

____

____

III. Read Galatians 5:22–26.

What did Paul mean by the "fruit" of the Spirit—the results of the Spirit, the traits of the Spirit, or something else? Explain.

____

____

____

Is there another kind of fruit that could be in this list? Why are these nine listed? What makes them important? Does this list contain everything the Spirit wants to do in our lives, or is there more? What difference does it make whether we understand the list as exhaustive (containing every way we should live) or representative (containing the *types* of ways we should live)?

Define each aspect of the fruit in your own words:

Love

Joy

Peace

Forbearance

Kindness

Goodness

Faithfulness

Gentleness

Self-control

Are the aspects of the fruit listed in some kind of important order? Explain.
How (if possible) would you rank them in order of importance?

Is it necessary for someone to be a believer and be filled with the Holy Spirit
to display love, joy, peace, or any of these other things? Why or why not?

Which aspect of the fruit of the Spirit is easiest for you to exhibit? Which
aspect is the most difficult for you to exhibit? Why do you think this is so?

Relating Fruit to Fruit

It is important for us to understand the fruit of the Spirit as a "package deal" rather than a list from which we can pick and choose. Part of doing this is recognizing the uniqueness and benefits of the aspects. For each aspect of the fruit of Spirit listed below, choose a physical fruit that corresponds to it and creatively explain why. (For example, love is like an apple because it is crisp to the senses.)

Love is like ____

because ____ .

Joy is like ____

because ____ .

Peace is like ____

because ____ .

Forbearance is like ____

because ____ .

Kindness is like ____

because ____ .

Goodness is like ____

because ____ .

Faithfulness is like ____

because ____.

Gentleness is like ____

because ____.

Self-control is like ____

because ____.

How does this activity offer insight into the fruit of the Spirit? Why might it be important for us to understand and remember the diversity of the fruit of the Spirit? What does it tell us about the character of Christians?

Why do men seem to struggle with some aspects of the fruit of the Spirit?

From your study today, what have you learned about the fruit of the Spirit? Which aspects of the fruit are you finding an increased interest in? Why?

Acts of the Flesh

Look back at Galatians 5:19–21 and rewrite it in your own words. Focus on using modern terms that describe the "acts of the flesh" listed.

What catches your attention after doing this rewrite? How are the struggles of people in Paul's day still a challenge for people in our day? How are some of these struggles particular problems for men in our society? Why do you think this is so? If Paul said plainly that those who live in this way will not inherit God's kingdom, why do some people persist in "fleshly" behavior?

If you were asked to give a short message to others on this part of the passage, what would be your main point? Why are verses 22–26 necessary to "complete the picture" and bring hope?

____

____

____

____

How can the other members of this group help you to live a life that is filled with the Spirit rather than focused on acts of the flesh?

____

____

____

____

Closing Prayer

Lord God, we have been shown the kind of character we need to have in these moments of study. We have fallen short in manifesting the fruit of the Spirit in our daily lives. Forgive us. We need your Holy Spirit's power to work within us, purging acts of the flesh and developing fruit that is pleasing to you. Help us to serve others in love as we walk in step with your Spirit. Amen. ∎